A

USEFUL

PUNCTUATION HANDBOOK

FOR ADULTS

I have had many years of experience in teaching adults and post-school learners in Adult Basic Education, Further Education and various other education settings. Almost universally, I have found that the two main problems affecting adults with poor literacy skills are learning how to use punctuation and learning how to spell. Some points of punctuation are trickier than others, and it is often hard to remember where to put an apostrophe, how to use speech marks and so on.

In this book, I have used the same approach as when I teach people face-to-face, and I hope that readers and users of "A Useful Punctuation Handbook for Adults" will enjoy having the next best thing to "personal tuition" as they work their way through the various rules of punctuation and emerge as better writers.

Help with spelling can be found in a separate book, "A Useful Spelling Handbook for Adults", and advice for dyslexic adults is provided in "A Useful Dyslexia Handbook for Adults".

Catherine Taylor

A

USEFUL

PUNCTUATION HANDBOOK

FOR ADULTS

Red Cat Publishing

Halifax

West Yorkshire

redcatpublishing@hotmail.com

A CIP catalogue record for this title is available from the British Library.

ISBN: 978-0-9565667-0-6

First published in 2010

Red Cat Publishing

Halifax
West Yorkshire
www.redcatpublishing.co.uk

Printed in Great Britain

DEDICATION

To Dave, for constant support, understanding,
encouragement and practical help.

To members of my family, again for their support,
encouragement and enthusiasm.

Also to my friends and colleagues for their interest,
encouragement and support.

CONTENTS

Page

1. What is punctuation?   11

2. Capital letters   17

3. Full stops   23

4. Question marks   26

5. Exclamation marks   27

6. Commas   28

7. Apostrophes   34

8. Quotation marks   39

9. Dashes, hyphens & brackets   44

10. Colons, semi-colons & ellipses   46

11. Paragraphs   48

12. Texting and word-processing   53

Answers   54

1. WHAT IS PUNCTUATION?

When people speak to each other, they normally communicate by using words with which to convey their thoughts and ideas. However, a closer look at spoken language shows us that this is by no means the full story. Listen to, and watch, anyone chatting. They will pause and hesitate while they consider something that they, or someone else, has said or is saying. They will add meaning to their words by using facial expression, gesture, and tone of voice. Sometimes their speech will run on and on where, ideally, they should stop or pause, but you will know what they mean.

People communicate through writing, as well as other non-verbal means such as art and music. Writing is also made up mainly of words. However, a string of letters cannot show the variations normally heard in speech, which are needed for full meaning and understanding. Instead we have to use a series of written marks along with the words, to clarify what we are saying in writing. This collection of marks is called 'punctuation'.

Exercise 1.1
Read the following, where no punctuation has been used:

it was a nice warm day the sun was shining and i decided to go for a walk in oaklands park with my dog ben come on ben i said lets put your lead on the dog jumped up barking excitedly his tail

11

wagging off we went down the road to the park straight away i spotted my friend james james i shouted its me what are you doing here he turned round and smiled what a nice surprise hows ben fine i answered where are you going im just on my way to the shop i need some milk bread a newspaper and a mobile topup if theyre open do you think they will be i dont know lets find out shall we what about ben its okay well come back to the park after the shop ben wont mind

What happened when you read this? How did it make you feel? You can perhaps see now why we need punctuation!

Here is a list of the marks of punctuation, showing what they are each used for, together with examples:

Punctuation mark	Name of punctuation mark	Where punctuation is used	Example
ABC	Capital letter	Begins a sentence. Used for special names of things.	It looks like rain. Today John went to see the Eiffel Tower.

.	Full stop	Ends a sentence which is a statement. Also used after certain abbreviations (shortened words).	He is due to arrive on Tuesday. Harry Jones Esq.
?	Question mark	Ends a sentence which is a question.	Would you like to see a film?
!	Exclamation mark	Ends a sentence which is an exclamation.	Watch out!
,	Comma	Separates part of a sentence.	I asked him to come over, and suggested that he bring a coat, walking boots, a rucksack and a map.

,	Apostrophe	Used to show that someone or something has ownership of someone or something else, i.e. a state of belonging. Shortens certain words and shows that a letter or letters has been missed out.	This is Tara's house. She's going on holiday, and we said we'd look after the cat. There'll be no problem. I'm quite happy to do it and he'll be all right.
"m"	Quotation marks	Show a quotation of exact words spoken.	"It's me," I said.

-	Dashes	Show a break in text.	My cat – a Siamese – is a fussy eater.
-	Hyphens	Link two words, or parts of words.	Co-operative.
(xx)	Brackets	Used to add information.	Mr Smith (the man next door) always waves to me.
:	Colon	Introduces information.	Bring the following items: boots, a rope, a waterproof coat and a map.
;	Semi-colon	Separates parts of a long sentence.	Go to the door; tell me what you can see.
…	Ellipses	Show that text is missing, or has ended prematurely.	Have you heard about…?

	Paragraph	The paragraph does not have a mark as such, but is laid out in a certain way. We begin a new paragraph when we begin a new topic in written text. A new paragraph starts on a new line, usually with an indentation.

2. CAPITAL LETTERS

Capital letters are used for:	<u>Examples</u>
Starting a sentence	The cat sat on the mat. He glared at me.
The word 'I' (also I've, I'm, I'd, I'll)	I think I should do this.
People's names and their titles	Joanne, Ali, Anne Frank, Tom Bennett, Mr Chan, Einstein, Billy the Kid, President Roosevelt, Mrs Jones, Inspector Morse, Ms Chloe Russell, Prime Minister, King Henry...
Special names of places	United Kingdom, Australia, Kashmir, Buckingham Palace, Lake Constance, the Alps, the Indian Ocean, London, Russia, Lilac Street, Netherfield College, Sainsbury's.
Days of the week, months of the year, special days	Sunday, Monday, June, July, Easter Sunday, Eid, Boxing Day, Diwali, Spring Holiday.
Nationalities	English, European, Russian, Asian,

	Egyptian, French, Chinese.
Languages	German, Urdu, Polish, Punjabi, English, Italian, Japanese.
Religions and religious descriptions	Christanity, Jewish, Islam, Buddhist.
Titles of books, songs, films, paintings etc. (main words only)	The Wind in the Willows. Lord of the Rings. The Prime of Miss Jean Brodie. Star Trek. Brief Encounter. The Laughing Cavalier. From a Distance. The X Factor.

Exercise 2.1

Re-write these sentences, using capital letters to begin them and for the words 'I', 'I've', etc.

a) i don't know where i've put my pen.
b) you want coffee, i want tea, he wants water, she wants milk.
c) i'm going into town. i can drop you off if you like.
d) the house is empty. i'd like to look at it. i'll book an appointment.
e) my car is old. i've had it for ten years.

f) it's very cold. the pond is frozen. it might snow.
g) do you think i look all right?
h) if we set off now, i could call at the shop.
i) there are a few things i need. i hope you don't mind.
j) i wish i could explain to you how i feel.

Exercise 2.2
Re-write these sentences, using capital letters for people's names and their titles.

a) My name is jack brown.
b) Are you the prime minister?
c) This is prince henry and princess rosalind.
d) Could I introduce you to the right honourable sir charles smith?
e) My cousin changed his name to richard archibald-hanson.
f) Are you mr and mrs slater?
g) my friends called their son simon oliver conan harry brendan davis.
h) sir cliff richard has had a wonderful career.
i) 'doctor who' has been on TV for many years.
j) The second man to set foot on the moon was buzz aldrin.

Exercise 2.3
Re-write these, using a capital letter for special names of places. Bear in mind that if a place name is used in a general way, you do not need a capital letter, for example "I am a student at Netherfield **College**. I go to **college** four days a week."

19

a) I lived in a house called honey cottage, at the end of a track called green lane.
b) The children went to a school in rushforth.
c) Have you been to the taj mahal?
d) I once climbed ben nevis.
e) Did you know that london is the capital city of england?
f) We were married at saint matilda's church in westcliffe.
g) I attended hadley community college, which was my local college.
h) I watched a TV programme about a remote village in the himalayas.
i) The train stops at lowbridge, cranley, hightown, and then goes through to southwell.
j) We have just crossed the border between england and wales.

Exercise 2.4
Fill in the gaps in these sentences, starting your answers with a capital letter.

a) My favourite day is _____.
b) I was born in the month of _____.
c) The weather is often cold in _____.
d) The 25th _____ is Christmas _____.
e) We give chocolate eggs at _____.
f) _____ _____ _____ is on the 1st January.
g) My Muslim friends are celebrating _____ today.

h) The 5th November is known as _____

_____ _____.

i) The hottest month of the year is usually

_____.

j) My favourite month is _____.

Exercise 2.5
Fill in the gaps, starting your answers with a capital letter.

a) I was born in France, and I speak _____.
b) I learned Norwegian because I wanted to work in _____.
c) Spaghetti and pizza are _____ dishes.
d) The main language spoken in the U.K. is

_____.

e) Three other languages spoken in the U.K. are

_____, _____ and _____.
f) The main language I speak is _____.
g) The Pyramids are a famous _____ sight.
h) If you come from Holland, you are said to be

_____.

i) Josh lives in the U.S.A., which means he is

_____.

j) If you come from Poland, you are likely to speak _____.

Exercise 2.6
Fill in the gaps, using a capital letter for the main words in these titles.

a) My favourite film is "_____".
b) May favourite book is "_____".

c) My favourite song is "_____".
d) The newspaper or magazine I read the most is
"_____".
e) My favourite TV programme is "_____".
f) Two games I enjoy playing are "_____" and
"_____".
g) Da Vinci painted a famous portrait of a woman
which he called "The _____ _____".

3. FULL STOPS (.)

Before working on full stops, it is important to know about sentences.
A sentence is a group of words that makes complete sense in itself. It begins with a capital letter and, if it is a statement, ends in a full stop.

Look at the following groups of words. Decide if each one makes complete sense in itself. If it helps, you can imagine that someone is *saying* the words to you.

a) I'm going to wash my car
b) My car
c) It's hot
d) There is no need for you to bring a coat because the weather is fine and warm and it's going to stay like that, according to the weather forecast
e) Whenever you see a pink elephant

a), c) and d) each make complete sense in themselves and are therefore sentences, which need to begin with a capital letter and end in a full stop.

Exercise 3.1
Decide which of the following are sentences. Put a full stop at the end if you think they are sentences, and a cross if you think they are not. If it helps, imagine that someone is *saying* the words to you.

a) I need a haircut

b) Although there was a large audience
c) Whenever I hear that tune
d) There are so many stars in the sky that it is impossible for anyone to count them
e) I like coffee
f) Driving towards the city centre
g) She says
h) This is one of the best books I have ever read, and I particularly enjoyed the ending where the two main characters make friends again
i) Stand at the top of the stairs
j) If ever you decide to buy a new computer

Exercise 3.2
In each of the following, there are two or more sentences. The number of sentences in each question is shown at the end. Write these out, putting in the full stops and a capital letter wherever one is needed.

a) on thursday I am flying to greece my aunt and uncle are already there (2)
b) when you get to dendale college, report to reception you will be directed to the board room mr mason will be waiting for you (3)
c) she has made an appointment with dr jones at hill top surgery it is on friday 3rd september (2)
d) this is a good film it's called "black saturday" my favourite actor is in it his name is jake grey (4)
e) my address is 23, oak street, duffield we went to live there in january before that I lived in nottingham it was hard getting ready to move

in december everyone else was celebrating
christmas (5)

Abbreviations

In the last exercise, **abbreviations** were used in
question b) and in question c).
An abbreviation is a shortened form of a word, such
as 'Dr' for 'Doctor' or 'Mr' for 'Mister'. These particular
abbreviations do not need to have a full stop at the
end, as their last letter is the same as the full version.
Abbreviated words with a final letter which is *not* the
same as that in the full version, e.g. 'Rev.' for
'Reverend', need a full stop at the end.

Exercise 3.3
Write out the abbreviations of these words, and put a
full stop at the end if this is needed.

    a) Avenue
    b) Street
    c) et cetera
    d) Honourable
    e) Road
    f) Drive
    g) Crescent
    h) Reverend
    i) Doctor
    j) Mister
    k) Mistress (which we now pronounce 'Missis')
    l) Major

4. QUESTION MARKS (?)

A question mark is used to show that a question is being asked. It is used *as an alternative to a full stop* at the end of a sentence which asks a question. If you look carefully at a question mark you will see that there is a full stop at its base.

Exercise 4.1
Decide which of the following sentences should end with a full stop, and which sentences should end with a question mark. Write in the full stop or question mark at the end of the sentence.

    a) Can you give me a lift into town, please
    b) I wanted to ask you a question
    c) I keep wondering if I ought to go
    d) Am I going mad
    e) Are you ready
    f) Could you deliver it the front door instead of the back one
    g) I'm not sure whether I prefer the green shirt or the blue one
    h) Why don't you buy both
    i) Would you please be quiet
    j) I am not very good at asking questions

Exercise 4.2
Make up six questions of your own. Put a question mark at the end of them.

5. EXCLAMATION MARKS (!)

An exclamation mark is used to show emphasis and express strong feeling. Like the questions mark, it is used as *an alternative to a full stop*. Again, if you look carefully at the exclamation mark, you will see that there is a full stop at its base.

Exercise 5.1
Decide which of the following sentences should end with a full stop, and which sentences should end with an exclamation mark. Write in the full stop or exclamation mark at the end of the sentence.

a) Get out
b) I don't know
c) There are no buses
d) Don't do that
e) Stand back
f) Come this way, please
g) Get out of the way, quick
h) I need to lie down
i) I don't feel well
j) Watch out

6. COMMAS (,)

Commas are used for separating parts of a sentence. This can be in any of the following situations:
- Marking a pause in a long sentence.
- Separating items in a list.
- Putting additional information into a sentence part way through it.
- Adding a question tag.
- Separating the different parts of an address.

Commas for marking a pause in a long sentence

Exercise 6.1
Read each of these sentences. Show where you should add a comma. There is one comma in each sentence which marks a pause.

a) Gill took the stage and sat down at the piano taking a series of deep breaths before she felt ready to begin.
b) There never seem to be enough hours in each day especially when you have lots of interesting hobbies like I do.
c) If you don't get your car repaired soon before long it will fall to pieces.
d) I made a really silly mistake while I was at work but I was brave enough to admit it to everyone.
e) I had planned to go on holiday this year for the first time in ages but I have had to pay for a lot of unexpected house repairs.

f) I could draw a map to show you where to go once you reach the city but it would be much better to borrow my satellite navigation system.

g) I read a good book over the weekend which was a really exciting story and I was so engrossed that I missed my favourite TV programme.

Commas for separating items in a list

Where you have a 'list' of items in a sentence, these need to be separated by using one comma after each item in the 'list'. Before the last 'item' it is usual to include the word 'and'. You do not need a comma before the word 'and' + the final item in the list. For example:

If you go to the shop we need some bread, butter, tea, coffee and sugar.

I go to work on Monday, Tuesday, Thursday, Friday and Saturday.

Exercise 6.2

Put the commas into these sentences where needed. Remember that you do not need to put a comma before the 'and' + the final item in the list.

a) I like to drink tea coffee hot chocolate spring water diet coke and milk.

b) The family who live next door to me have a dog a cat two rabbits some tropical fish two ponies four geese and a lot of hens.

c) You will go past a garage a row of shops some traffic lights a cinema a pelican crossing and a swimming pool.
d) The market is open on Mondays Tuesdays Fridays and Saturdays.
e) The dark nights the cold weather the bare trees and the lack of outdoor activities all make me dislike the winter.
f) I feel happier in the summer when the days are long the sun shines there are lots of flowers and I can get out more.
g) My favourite foods are salad chicken baked potatoes all vegetables and salmon.
h) The injured man had a broken leg two cracked ribs cuts bruises and a sprained ankle.
i) The only change I have is two pound coins five twenty pence pieces six ten pence pieces and a lot of copper.
j) Policemen firemen postmen bus drivers and nurses all wear a uniform.

Commas for adding information

A pair of commas is used to put additional information into a sentence. For example:
The house, which was very old, needed a lot of repairs.
My father, who was born in London, has travelled all over the world.
You can see where the commas should go by checking if the sentence still makes sense when the additional information is removed from it. For example:

The house, which was very old, needed a lot of repairs.
The house needed a lot of repairs.

My father, who was born in London, has travelled all over the world.
My father has travelled all over the world.

These sentences still make sense without the additional information – in the first sentence 'which was very old', and in the second sentence 'who was born in London'.

Exercise 6.3
Put a pair of commas into each of these sentences around the added information.

   a) Mr Ansell who has a very nice car often walks to work.
   b) The route along a narrow winding track is the quickest way to get there.
   c) My car the best in the range is my pride and joy.
   d) London the capital city of England has many fine historic buildings.
   e) The hotel which was featured on TV has everything you could wish for.

Exercise 6.4
Replace 'xxxx' in these sentences with your additional information, putting in a pair of commas where needed.

a) My friend xxxx asked if I'd like to go with her.
b) My dog xxxx doesn't like meeting new people.
c) These shoes xxxx are my favourite pair.
d) These instructions xxxx are written in a way that is hard to understand.
e) My job xxxx is very interesting.

Commas for adding a question tag

When we turn a statement into a question by adding a 'tag', a comma is needed. For example:
Statement: **It's a lovely day.**
Question: **It's a lovely day, isn't it?**
Statement: **The sky is very blue today.**
Question: **The sky is very blue today, isn't it?**

Exercise 6.5
Add a comma, capital letters and a question mark where needed in each of these sentences.

a) It's cold isn't it
b) You don't mind do you
c) You know I want to go to greece don't you
d) I don't suppose you've seen ben have you
e) The queen lives in buckingham palace doesn't she

Commas for separating the different parts of an address

When you are writing an address, commas need to be placed after the house name or number and after

each line in the address, *apart from the final line where a full stop is needed.*
For example:
16, Fountain Road,
Eastway,
Yourtown,
YR5 7ST.

Exercise 6.6
Add commas, capital letters and a full stop where needed in the following.

    a) This is my address: 22 drake road nether bridge halford hf8 4pt

    b) I live at 5 west street hightown ht6 3ab

    c) I attend spring vale college spring vale road springtown sp2 3bm

7. APOSTROPHES (')

There are two main uses of the apostrophe. These are:

1. To show that a letter, or letters, is/are missing from a shortened word.
Examples:
'I'll go' is short for **'I will go'**. The apostrophe shows that the letters **'wi'** are missing.
'He's wrong' is short for **'He is wrong'**. The apostrophe shows that the letter **'i'** is missing.
NOTE: 'won't' is short for 'will not', and 'shan't' is short for 'shall not'.

2. To show that someone or something belongs to someone or something else.
Examples:
Ali's daughter is seven years old today = The daughter belonging to Ali is seven years old today.
The caravan's windows were broken = The windows belonging to the caravan were broken.

Let us look at these in turn.

Apostrophe to show a missing letter or missing letters from a word

Exercise 7.1
Write out the apostrophe words in full.

a) I think I'll go to bed.

b) I can't make up my mind.
c) Don't go.
d) There's not much time.
e) I won't go.
f) I shouldn't think so.
g) I wouldn't know,
h) I shan't tell you.
i) He couldn't come.
j) I'm new here.

Exercise 7.2
Shorten the words in bold type to one word using an apostrophe.
a) I **did not** know that.
b) **We are** going on holiday.
c) **I have** been away.
d) I **could not** do it.
e) **It is** time to go.
f) I think **she is** cute.
g) I think **you will** know her.
h) **We have** forgotten something.
i) If he can, **he will** get here.
j) **They have** been and gone.

Apostrophe to show that someone or something belongs to someone or something else

The examples already shown refer to singular words (where there is only one 'owner'). In this case we place the apostrophe *before* the 's'.
'The caravan's windows were broken' refers to one caravan only. However, if we were making the same remark about *more than one* caravan (a plural

word), the apostrophe is placed *after* the 's', for example, '**The three caravans' windows were broken**'.

The general rule is that if the 'owner' is singular (just one), the apostrophe goes *before* the 's', and if the 'owners' are plural (more than one), the apostrophe goes *after* the 's'. However, there are a few plural words which look like singular words, e.g. men, women, and in this case we treat the plural word as a singular word, for example 'the women's athletics event'.

Another thing to note is that there is no apostrophe is these words:
his = belonging to him
hers = belonging to her
theirs = belonging to them
its = belonging to it
yours = belonging to you
ours = belonging to us

Exercise 7.3
Put the apostrophes into these words where they are needed, to show *belonging*.

   a) Pauls hair is very long
   b) The chefs skills are second to none.
   c) The books title is misleading.
   d) I like driving my mothers car.
   e) Have you ever been to one of Dee Youngs performances?
   f) We are nearly at our journeys end.

g) The managers rooms have been reserved.
h) I have received the candidates references.
i) The mens race is about to begin.
j) The doctors surgery is closed.
k) I enjoy reading womens magazines.
l) My granddad belonged to a Gentlemens Club.
m) Percy Shaw invented reflecting road studs after seeing how cats eyes lit up in the dark.
n) I don't understand that mans point of view.
o) All the workers wages are really good.

Exercise 7.4

Complete the gaps in these sentences. Remember that no apostrophe is needed in the words *his, hers, theirs, its* (* see next exercise), *yours, ours.*

a) The book was given to John, so I think it is

_____.

b) This piece of land is shown on our deeds, so it must be _____.

c) A tiger can easily be recognised by the marks on _____ coat.

d) I found this coat in my car after giving you a lift, so I think it must be _____.

e) Holly insists that the trainers are _____.

f) The twins told me that the car is _____ to share at.

Exercise 7.5

Fill in the gaps with either its or it's. Remember:

its = belonging to it
it's = it is

a) I think ___ going to rain.
b) ___ the best thing I ever did.
c) The dog is wagging ___ tail.
d) ___ only 8 o'clock.
e) Do you know what time ___ starting?
f) Each house has ___ own garden.
g) I think ___ going to be good.
h) The school has ___ own swimming pool.
i) A computer has ___ uses.
j) A good supermarket knows the needs of ___ customers.

8. QUOTATION MARKS ("xx")

Speech marks

Quotation marks are used to show the exact words that someone has said; that is, to show a direct quotation. These marks are often called **speech** marks. They may be shown as either 'single' or 'double' speech marks. For example:
'Too true,' I said.
"Too true," he replied.

Look at a range of books and magazines, and you will see that some publications use 'single' speech marks, and others use "double" speech marks, according to the preferred publishing style.
Speech marks go around the whole of the words spoken, including any punctuation that is part of the speech. The 'opening' speech marks (") are used at the beginning of the speech to show that it is open, and the 'closing' speech marks (") are used right at the end of the speech and its accompanying punctuation, to show that the speech has closed.
"It's going to be hot today," Jake said.
"Have you seen that film?" I asked.
Annie turned to me and shouted, **"Be careful!"**

You can also interrupt the speech partway through, by commenting on what someone has said. For example:
"I think," said my brother, **"we should buy a new car for the journey."**

The first word of every new speech made by a new speaker *always* begins on a new line. However, it can be very confusing knowing where to use capital letters with speech marks. The first word of every new speech *always* begins with a capital letter. For example:

"What is your name?"
"My name is a secret."
"Won't you tell me?"
"Certainly not."

If speech is interrupted partway through with a comment, and then continues, a comma is used after the first part of the speech, and another comma after the comment. For example:

"I think," he said, "it's time we were going home."

However, if speech is followed by a comment which ends the sentence, a comma is used after the speech, and a full stop is used after the comment. For example:

"I don't know," she said.
The exception to this is when the speech finishes with a question mark or exclamation mark:
"Watch out!" he shouted.
"Could I have some water, please?" she asked.

Finally, if speech is interrupted partway through with a comment which will end the sentence *and this is followed by further speech from the same speaker,* then a comma is used after the first part of the speech, a full stop is used after the comment, and

the continuing speech is treated as a new speech beginning with a capital letter but continuing on the same line. For example:
"I don't know where my keys are," my mum said. "Have you got a spare set?"

Exercise 8.1
Put speech marks into the following. Remember they are placed around the actual quotation (or the words said) along with any punctuation that goes with the speech.

    a) Do you want a lift? he asked.
    b) No thank you, I said.
    c) Abi commented to me, It's very cold today.
    d) My computer's not working, the woman said.
    e) Vikki said, There aren't many people here.
    f) He hesitated before saying to me, We'll have to set on more staff.

Exercise 8.2
Now put speech marks, commas and capital letters into these sentences.

    a) Your car needs cleaning the boy whispered.
    b) You can't come in here the manager said.
    c) Emma looked at me and said you haven't a leg to stand on.
    d) The telephone's ringing I pointed out.
    e) Aren't you going to answer it I asked.
    f) My mother said it's your birthday next week.

Now put speech marks and any other punctuation into these sentences.

a) Rebecca I said you're wearing a dress just like Jessica's

b) If you go shopping Josh said would you bring me a newspaper and a bar of chocolate

c) Don't do that I shouted you'll break it

d) The weather is fine she said for ducks and fish

e) You might be right he said after all

f) Shall I turn on the light I suggested then we'll be able to see better

g) Sorry I told him I'm not interested

h) Where there's muck the old man said there's always money.

i) I can't see properly I told the optician I think I need a new pair of glasses

j) Well well Chloe said what do we have here

Other uses of quotation marks

Quotation marks are also used to quote the exact words that someone has said when we are referring to their speech indirectly, or reporting on their speech. In these cases, the punctuation is placed outside the quotation marks. For example:

Emma was telling me about her holiday. She said everything had gone wrong "from the moment she boarded the plane".

Quotation marks are used to quote the exact words extracted from other sources such as a book, film or radio programme and so on. For example:

The author referred to the main character as **"a rebel without a cause"**.

In the film, Jack told Jill that she must **"walk faster if we are to get there before dark"**.

Exercise 8.4
Put the quotation marks into these sentences.

a) The man told me he was an old hand at sailing a boat.
b) The writer tells us that Rigby's best ever meal was eaten on the cliff top.
c) He explained that the music is a variant of jazz mixed with a bit of classical.
d) I remember, as a toddler, telling my mother that I was a poor little girl.
e) The dentist told me I would have a smile like a million dollars.
f) When your scores are equal you are said to have a draw.
g) My grandmother told me there was a pot of gold at the end of the rainbow.

9. DASHES, HYPHENS & BRACKETS (-)

Dashes

A dash shows a break in text. If the text is to continue after the break, a further dash is needed. Dashes should be used sparingly, as very often a different punctuation mark would be more suitable. Examples:
My father – the man in the photo – was a very strong man.
Tennis – which I play regularly during the summer – is a wonderful sport.
(In each of these sentences we could equally have used a pair of commas or brackets.)

Hyphens

The hyphen is used to link two words, or two parts of words. Examples:
My grandfather was a self-made man.
Apples are a year-round fruit.
The hyphen can also be used when a word is broken by reaching the end of a line. The hyphen must be shown at the end of a syllable and at the end of the line, *not* the beginning of the next one.

Brackets

Brackets are used to add information. There is one 'opening' bracket, and one 'closing' bracket. Examples:
My neighbour (Jo) is always very kind to me.

The president (born in 1950) has had a fascinating life.
(Again, in each of these sentences we could equally have used a pair of dashes or a pair of commas.)

Exercise 9.1
In each of these sentences an 'X', or a pair of 'X's, is shown. State if you would use a hyphen, a pair of brackets or a pair of dashes.

a) My father X the owner of the factory X is the best manager I know.
   (hyphen/dashes/brackets)
b) He is in his mid X forties.
   (hyphen/dashes/brackets)
c) Potatoes X my favourite food X can be cooked in a variety of ways. (hyphen/dashes/brackets)
d) I was talking to Mr King X the landlord X last night. (hyphen/dashes/brackets)
e) My grandfather was a soldier in the First World War X 1914-1918 X.
   (hyphen/dashes/brackets)
f) I have a multi X fuel burning stove.
   (hyphen/dashes/brackets)
g) Logs X which are in plentiful supply X are a cheap form of fuel. (hyphen/dashes/brackets)

10. COLONS, SEMI-COLONS & ELLIPSES (: ; ...)

Colons

A colon is a mark of *introduction.* Look at the
following examples:
**I have used a colon above to introduce some
examples. Here they are:**
**Can you please bring the following items to your
exam:**

> **pencil**
> **eraser**
> **ruler**
> **calculator**

**The woman stared at me and said loudly: "I think
I know you."**

Semi-colons

A semi-colon separates parts of a long sentence. It is
more emphatic than a comma, but not as emphatic
as a full stop. Examples:
**I've bought a pair of blue shoes; normally I only
wear black.**
**I never tell anyone my password; it would be a
foolish thing to do.**

Ellipses

An ellipses is shown by a series of three dots, and
shows that text is missing, or has ended prematurely.
Examples:

**She went to the station, got on the train, found a
seat and...well, you know the rest.
"James," I said, "can you please put that on
the..."**

Exercise 10.1
In each of the following sentences an 'X' is shown.
State if you would use a colon, semi-colon or ellipses
where the 'X' is.

a) Ella is my half-sister X but no doubt you can
see that. (colon/semi-colon/ellipses)
b) I tried to imagine the room painted in different
colours X blue, pink, beige, lilac, white, cream,
pale green. (colon/semi-colon/ellipses)
c) The months of the year are: January,
February, March, April X and so on, till
December. (colon/semi-colon/ellipses)
d) I can't tell you X that is the end of the story.
(colon/semi-colon/ellipses)
e) Did you know that I'm X no, I don't suppose
you do. (colon/semi-colon/ellipses)
f) The buffet had sandwiches, pies, French
bread, salad, samosas, cold meats, cheese X
everything you could think of. (colon/semi-
colon/ellipses)
g) The winners of the show are X Rebecca,
Stephanie and Simon. (colon/semi-
colon/ellipses)
h) I can't do it X you'll have to believe me.
(colon/semi-colon/ellipses)

11. PARAGRAPHS

A paragraph is a group of sentences dealing with one topic only. Splitting written text into paragraphs helps you to read the text more easily. For example, look at the following piece:

As usual, I set off to take my dog for a walk this morning, to the field where we normally go. I let the dog off the lead. I was halfway across the field when I noticed, to my absolute horror, that the farmer had put a big bull in the field. I saw the bull walking towards me. The dog ran off. I let him go, which I felt was the safest thing to do. Quickly – but not too quickly – I walked towards the wall at the edge of the field, intending to climb over. It was then I saw that the farmer had put up some barbed wire fencing. The bull was getting closer, and moving faster. I scrambled under the barbed wire and over the wall, and I tore my hand on the barbed wire and scraped my knee on the stone wall. To my relief the dog came back and we hurried home. I went upstairs to the bathroom to get some plasters and antiseptic from the cabinet. I could not believe it when the cabinet fell off the wall and hit my head really hard. At that moment the phone rang. I ran downstairs to answer it. In my haste, I tripped over some things which had been left on the staircase, fell down the stairs and sprained my ankle. I searched for a bandage to put on my ankle, and couldn't find one, so I went to the supermarket. The supermarket did not sell bandages so instead I had to go to the chemist. That is why I am so late for work today.

It is likely that you started off by finding the story interesting, but soon you stopped because you could not be bothered reading it, or felt daunted by the way the text was laid out.

Try reading the same piece with the paragraphs put in, which should be much easier:

As usual, I set off to take my dog for a walk this morning, to the field where we normally go. I let the dog off the lead. I was halfway across the field when I noticed, to my absolute horror, that the farmer had put a big bull in the field.

I saw the bull walking towards me. The dog ran off. I let him go, which I felt was the safest thing to do. Quickly – but not too quickly – I walked towards the wall at the edge of the field, intending to climb over. It was then I saw that the farmer had put up some barbed wire fencing.

The bull was getting closer, and moving faster. I scrambled under the barbed wire and over the wall, and I tore my hand on the barbed wire and scraped my knee on the stone wall. To my relief the dog came back and we hurried home.

I went upstairs to the bathroom to get some plasters and antiseptic from the cabinet. I could not believe it when the cabinet fell off the wall and hit my head really hard.

At that moment the phone rang. I ran downstairs to answer it. In my haste, I tripped over some things which had been left on the staircase, fell down the stairs and sprained my ankle.

I searched for a bandage to put on my ankle, and couldn't find one, so I went to the supermarket. The supermarket did not sell bandages so instead I had to go to the chemist.

That is why I am so late for work today.

There are no rules about how short or long a paragraph should be, or how many sentences it should contain. You should start a new paragraph when you start a new topic.

In most publications, a new paragraph is shown by 'indenting' the first line of the paragraph – that is, it starts a little further in than the other lines. The first line of the chapter, or the beginning of an article, is not normally 'indented'.

In more modern publications, you may see new paragraphs shown by placing a blank line between paragraphs.

Exercise 11.1
Show where the new paragraphs should start in this piece of text. Remember, you use a new paragraph where there is a new topic.

Have you ever moved house? No? I have, several times, and I always wonder if I am mad to take on such a project. I will tell you why. First of all, if you are buying a new property, you have to choose the house you want, which can take weeks or even months. Then, although the house has been put up for sale at a certain price, it is expected that you will make an offer. You decide how much you would *really* like to pay, put in your offer, and wait to see if it is accepted. Sometimes you have to increase the offer you have made, perhaps more than once. If you are selling a house at the same time, you have to have it valued, choose an estate agent, put it on the market, wait for the viewers to turn up…but we won't go into that. Okay, let's assume that everything's going forward, you've agreed a final price on the house you are buying, and the legal aspects are going as smoothly as can be expected. There are many letters to answer, phone calls to make, e-mails to send, price adjustments regarding the condition of the house and the fixtures and fittings. As the big day approaches you have to pack up the entire contents of your home. You find things you thought you had lost. You need to throw away lots of rubbish. You have to decide what you are taking with you, and what you will get rid of. Eventually you are living out of boxes, with only the barest minimum of things not packed. On the day of moving it is normal practice for you, your buyer and the person you are buying from all to move on the same day, so things must be planned with military precision. You can only hope that everything is all cleared out at your new home, and that it has been cleaned ready for you to move in. Luckily, your removal men arrive on time, and you watch your old house getting more and more empty. By the end of the day everything has been shifted, and you sit at your new place amongst the boxes, wondering where you will put everything. You are hungry and tired, but you feel much too scruffy in your old clothes to go out for a meal, and you haven't a clue where to find some clean ones. You don't even know how to turn the hot water system on. The most important thing is to sleep, so from out of the chaos you manage to put up the bed and find some sheets and a quilt. Your head hits the pillow and you sigh gratefully – rest at last! However, you can hear all kinds of strange noises and you don't know what they are, so you lie awake with your brain turning somersaults. Eventually sleep overtakes you, and you have some vivid dreams - wondering if you have done the right thing, missing your old bedroom, tossing and turning, waking at times disturbed by the strange noises. The next morning the sunlight pours through the window (where there are no curtains yet) and you wake up and stretch, wondering where you are. Then you remember, and happily you jump out of bed, knowing there is a long day and some hard work ahead. By the time evening comes, your new house is beginning to look like a home, and you can shower and change, ready to go out for a nice meal to celebrate. You look around proudly at your new house, remembering all the effort you have had to make, and suddenly you *know* it has all been worth it!

12. TEXTING AND WORD-PROCESSING

Sending text messages by mobile phone has given us almost a new language as we seek out ways to shorten the message so that it will fit into the space of one text. For example, we might write 'C U 4 lunch' instead of 'See you for lunch'. Text language can be creative, money saving and fun. It is very important, however, not to let text-speak creep into your written documents or notes which you might send to someone! They can make written text very difficult to read and, quite frankly, are often a mess.

When using a computer word-processor, the checking facility will flag up any errors you have made with spelling, punctuation and grammar. A word of warning is to check through the correction it has suggested, rather than trust that it will automatically be correct. The spell-check and grammar-check *offer you a list of corrections* from which to choose the right answer. If you are writing for your job, or if you are a student handing in assignments, it is important that you have a good working knowledge of spelling, grammar and punctuation, so that you *know* what is, and what is not, correct. *See the word-processor as a helpful tool, or a servant – but do not let it become your master!*

ANSWERS

Exercise 2.1
   a) I don't know where I've put my pen.
   b) You want coffee, I want tea, he wants water, she wants milk.
   c) I'm going into town. I can drop you off if you like.
   d) The house is empty. I'd like to look at it. I'll book an appointment.
   e) My car is old. I've had it for ten years.
   f) It's very cold. The pond is frozen. It might snow.
   g) Do you think I look all right?
   h) If we set off now, I could call at the shop.
   i) There are a few things I need. I hope you don't mind.
   j) I wish I could explain to you how I feel.

Exercise 2.2
   a) My name is Jack Brown.
   b) Are you the Prime Minister?
   c) This is Prince Henry and Princess Rosalind.
   d) Could I introduce you to the Right Honourable Sir Charles Smith?
   e) My cousin changed his name to Richard Archibald-Hanson.
   f) Are you Mr and Mrs Slater?
   g) My friends called their son Simon Oliver Conan Harry Brendan Davis.
   h) Sir Cliff Richard has had a wonderful career.
   i) 'Doctor Who' has been on TV for many years.

j) The second man to set foot on the moon was Buzz Aldrin.

Exercise 2.3
a) I lived in a house called Honey Cottage, at the end of a track called Green Lane.
b) The children went to a school in Rushforth.
c) Have you been to the Taj Mahal?
d) I once climbed Ben Nevis.
e) Did you know that London is the capital city of England?
f) We were married at Saint Matilda's church in Westcliffe.
g) I attended Hadley Community College, which was my local college.
h) I watched a TV programme about a remote village in the Himalayas.
i) The train stops at Lowbridge, Cranley, Hightown, and then goes through to Southwell.
j) We have just crossed the border between England and Wales.

Exercise 2.4
a) My favourite day is *(open answer beginning with a capital letter)*.
b) I was born in the month of *(open answer beginning with a capital letter)*.
c) The weather is often cold in *(open answer beginning with a capital letter)*.
d) The 25th December is Christmas Day.
e) We give chocolate eggs at Easter.
f) New Years Day is on the 1st January.

g) My Muslim friends are celebrating Eid today.
h) The 5th November is known as Guy Fawkes Night **or** Bonfire Night **or** Plot Night.
i) The hottest month of the year is usually *(open answer beginning with a capital letter).*
j) My favourite month is *(open answer beginning with a capital letter).*

Exercise 2.5
a) I was born in France, and I speak French.
b) I learned Norwegian because I wanted to work in Norway.
c) Spaghetti and pizza are Italian dishes.
d) The main language spoken in the U.K. is English.
e) Three other languages spoken in the U.K. are *(open answer, e.g. Welsh, Urdu, Gaelic etc.)*
f) The main language I speak is *(open answer beginning with a capital letter).*
g) The Pyramids are a famous Egyptian sight.
h) If you come from Holland, you are said to be Dutch.
i) Josh lives in the U.S.A., which means he is American.
j) If you come from Poland, you are likely to speak Polish.

Exercise 2.6
Open answers beginning with capital letters.
g) The Mona Lisa.

Exercise 3.1
a) I need a haircut.
b) Although there was a large audience x
c) Whenever I hear that tune x
d) There are so many stars in the sky that it is impossible for anyone to count them.
e) I like coffee.
f) Driving towards the city centre x
g) She says x
h) This is one of the best books I have ever read, and I particularly enjoyed the ending where the two main characters make friends again.
i) Stand at the top of the stairs x
j) If ever you decide to buy a new computer x

Exercise 3.2
a) Thursday I am flying to Greece. My aunt and uncle are already there.
b) When you get to Dendale College, report to Reception. You will be directed to the Board Room. Mr Mason will be waiting for you.
c) She has made an appointment with Dr Jones at Hill Top Surgery. It is on Friday 3rd September.
d) This is a good film. It's called "Black Saturday". My favourite actor is in it. His name is Jake Grey.
e) My address is 23, Oak Street, Duffield. We went to live there in January. Before that I lived in Nottingham. It was hard getting ready to move in December. Everyone else was celebrating Christmas.

Exercise 3.3
a) Ave
b) St
c) Etc.
d) Hon.
e) Rd
f) Dr.
g) Cres.
h) Rev.
i) Dr
j) Mr
k) Mrs
l) Maj.

Exercise 4.1
  a) Can you give me a lift into town, please?
  b) I wanted to ask you a question.
  c) I keep wondering if I ought to go.
  d) Am I going mad?
  e) Are you ready?
  f) Could you deliver it the front door instead of the back one?
  g) I'm not sure whether I prefer the green shirt or the blue one.
  h) Why don't you buy both?
  i) Would you please be quiet?
  j) I am not very good at asking questions.

Exercise 4.2
(Open answers ending with question marks)

Exercise 5.1
  a) Get out!
  b) I don't know.
  c) There are no buses.
  d) Don't do that!
  e) Stand back!
  f) Come this way, please.
  g) Get out of the way, quick!
  h) I need to lie down.
  i) I don't feel well.
  j) Watch out!

Exercise 6.1
a) Gill took the stage and sat down at the piano, taking a series of deep breaths before she felt ready to begin.

b) There never seem to be enough hours in each day, especially when you have lots of interesting hobbies like I do.
c) If you don't get your car repaired soon, before long it will fall to pieces.
d) I made a really silly mistake while I was at work, but I was brave enough to admit it to everyone.
e) I had planned to go on holiday this year for the first time in ages, but I have had to pay for a lot of unexpected house repairs.
f) I could draw a map to show you where to go once you reach the city, but it would be much better to borrow my satellite navigation system.
g) I read a good book over the weekend which was a really exciting story, and I was so engrossed that I missed my favourite TV programme.

Exercise 6.2

a) I like to drink tea, coffee, hot chocolate, spring water, diet coke and milk.
b) The family who live next door to me have a dog, a cat, two rabbits, some tropical fish, two ponies, four geese and a lot of hens.
c) You will go past a garage, a row of shops, some traffic lights, a cinema, a pelican crossing and a swimming pool.
d) The market is open on Mondays, Tuesdays, Fridays and Saturdays.

e) The dark nights, the cold weather, the bare trees and the lack of outdoor activities all make me dislike the winter.

f) I feel happier in the summer when the days are long, the sun shines, there are lots of flowers and I can get out more.

g) My favourite foods are salad, chicken, baked potatoes, all vegetables and salmon.

h) The injured man had a broken leg, two cracked ribs, cuts, bruises and a sprained ankle.

i) The only change I have is two pound coins, five twenty pence pieces, six ten pence pieces and a lot of copper.

j) Policemen, firemen, postmen, bus drivers and nurses all wear a uniform.

Exercise 6.3

a) Mr Ansell, who has a very nice car, often walks to work.

b) The route, along a narrow winding track, is the quickest way to get there.

c) My car, the best in the range, is my pride and joy.

d) London, the capital city of England, has many fine historic buildings.

e) The hotel, which was featured on TV, has everything you could wish for.

Exercise 6.4

a) My friend, *(open)*, asked if I'd like to go with her.

b) My dog, *(open)*, doesn't like meeting new people.
c) These shoes, *(open)*, are my favourite pair.
d) These instructions, *(open)*, are written in a way that is hard to understand.
e) My job, *(open)*, is very interesting.

Exercise 6.5

f) It's cold, isn't it?
g) You don't mind, do you?
h) You know I want to go to Greece, don't you?
i) I don't suppose you've seen Ben, have you?
j) The queen lives in Buckingham Palace, doesn't she?

Exercise 6.6

d) This is my address: 22 Drake Road, Nether Bridge, Halford, HF8 4PT.
e) I live at 5, West Street, Hightown, HT6 3AB.
f) I attend Spring Vale College, Spring Vale Road, Springtown, SP2 3BM.

Exercise 7.1

a) I think I will go to bed.
b) I can not *(or cannot)* make up my mind.
c) Do not go.
d) There is not much time.
e) I will not go.
f) I should not think so.
g) I would not know,
h) I shall not tell you.
i) He could not come.
j) I am new here.

i)   "I can't see properly," I told the optician. "I think I need a new pair of glasses."
j)   "Well, well," Chloe said. "What do we have here?"

Exercise 8.4
a)   The man told me he was "an old hand" at sailing a boat.
b)   The writer tells us that Rigby's "best ever meal" was eaten on the cliff top.
c)   He explained that the music is "a variant of jazz mixed with a bit of classical".
d)   I remember, as a toddler, telling my mother that I was a "poor little girl".
e)   The dentist told me I would have "a smile like a million dollars".
f)   When your scores are equal you are said to have a "draw".
g)   My grandmother told me there was "a pot of gold at the end of the rainbow".

Exercise 9.1
a)   My father - the owner of the factory - is the best manager I know. (dashes, but could also be commas or brackets)
b)   He is in his mid-forties. (hyphen)
c)   Potatoes - my favourite food - can be cooked in a variety of ways. (dashes, but could also be commas)
d)   I was talking to Mr King (the landlord) last night. (brackets, but could also be commas)
e)   My grandfather was a soldier in the First World War (1914-1918). (brackets)

Exercise 7.2
a)   didn't know that.
b)   We're going on holiday.
c)   I've been away.
d)   I couldn't do it.
e)   It's time to go.
f)   I think she's cute.
g)   I think you'll know her.
h)   We've forgotten something.
i)   If he can, he'll get here.
j)   They've been and gone.

Exercise 7.3
a)   Paul's hair is very long
b)   The chef's skills are second to none. *(If there was more than one chef, the apostrophe would go after the 's'.)*
c)   The book's title is misleading.
d)   I like driving my mother's car.
e)   Have you ever been to one of Dee Young's performances?
f)   We are nearly at our journey's end.
g)   The managers' rooms have been reserved. *(If there was only one manager, the apostrophe would go before the 's'.)*
h)   I have received the candidate's references. *(If there was more than candidate, the apostrophe would go after the 's'.)*
i)   The men's race is about to begin.
j)   The doctor's surgery is closed. *(If there was more than one doctor, the apostrophe would go after the 's'.)*

k) I enjoy reading women's magazines.
l) My granddad belonged to a Gentlemen's Club.
m) Percy Shaw invented reflecting road studs after seeing how cats' eyes lit up in the dark.
n) I don't understand that man's point of view.
o) All the workers' wages are really good.

Exercise 7.4
a) The book was given to John, so I think it is his.
b) This piece of land is shown on our deeds, so it must be ours.
c) A tiger can easily be recognised by the marks on its coat.
d) I found this coat in my car after giving you a lift, so I think it must be yours.
e) Holly insists that the trainers are hers.
f) The twins told me that the car is theirs to share at.

Exercise 7.5
a) I think it's going to rain.
b) It's the best thing I ever did.
c) The dog is wagging its tail.
d) It's only 8 o'clock.
e) Do you know what time it's starting?
f) Each house has its own garden.
g) I think it's going to be good.
h) The school has its own swimming pool.
i) A computer has its uses.
j) A good supermarket knows the needs of its customers.

Exercise 8.1
a) "Do you want a lift?" he asked.
b) "No thank you," I said.
c) Abi commented to me, "It's very cold today."
d) "My computer's not working," the woman said.
e) Vikki said, "There aren't many people here."
f) He hesitated before saying to me, "We'll have to set on more staff."

Exercise 8.2
a) "Your car needs cleaning," the boy whispered.
b) "You can't come in here," the manager said.
c) Emma looked at me and said, "You haven't a leg to stand on."
d) "The telephone's ringing," I pointed out.
e) "Aren't you going to answer it?" I asked.
f) My mother said, "It's your birthday next week."

Exercise 8.3
a) "Rebecca," I said, "you're wearing a dress just like Jessica's."
b) "If you go shopping," Josh said, "would you bring me a newspaper and a bar of chocolate?"
c) "Don't do that!" I shouted. "You'll break it!"
d) "The weather is fine," she said, "for ducks and fish."
e) "You might be right," he said, "after all."
f) "Shall I turn on the light?" I suggested. "Then we'll be able to see better."
g) "Sorry," I told him. "I'm not interested."
h) "Where there's muck," the old man said, "there's always money."

f) I have a multi-fuel burning stove. (hyphen)
g) Logs - which are in plentiful supply - are a cheap form of fuel. (dashes, but could also be commas)

Exercise 10.1
a) Ella is my half-sister; but no doubt you can see that. (semi-colon)
b) I tried to imagine the room painted in different colours: blue, pink, beige, lilac, white, cream, pale green. (colon)
c) The months of the year are: January, February, March, April…and so on, till December. (ellipses)
d) I can't tell you; that is the end of the story. (semi-colon)
e) Did you know that I'm…no, I don't suppose you do. (ellipses)
f) The buffet had sandwiches, pies, French bread, salad, samosas, cold meats, cheese…everything you could think of. (ellipses)
g) The winners of the show are: Rebecca, Stephanie and Simon. (colon)
h) I can't do it; you'll have to believe me. (semi-colon)

Exercise 11.1
Have you ever moved house? No? I have, several times, and I always wonder if I am mad to take on such a project. I will tell you why.

First of all, if you are buying a new property, you have to choose the house you want, which can take weeks or even months. Then, although the house has been put up for sale at a certain price, it is expected that you will make an offer. You decide how much you would *really* like to pay, put in your offer, and wait to see if it is accepted. Sometimes you have to increase the offer you have made, perhaps more than once. If you are selling a house at the same time, you have to have it valued, choose an estate agent, put it on the market, wait for the viewers to turn up…but we won't go into that.

Okay, let's assume that everything's going forward, you've agreed a final price on the house you are buying, and the legal aspects are going as smoothly as can be expected. There are many letters to answer, phone calls to make, e-mails to send, price adjustments regarding the condition of the house and the fixtures and fittings. As the big day approaches you have to pack up the entire contents of your home. You find things you thought you had lost. You need to throw away lots of rubbish. You have to decide what you are taking with you, and what you will get rid of. Eventually you are living out of boxes, with only the barest minimum of things not packed.

On the day of moving it is normal practice for you, your buyer and the person you are buying from all to move on the same day, so things must be planned with military precision. You can only hope that everything is all cleared out at your new home, and that it has been cleaned ready for you to move in. Luckily, your removal men arrive on time, and you watch your old house getting more and more empty.

By the end of the day everything has been shifted, and you sit at your new place amongst the boxes, wondering where you will put everything. You are hungry and tired, but you feel much too scruffy in your old clothes to go out for a meal, and you haven't a clue where to find some clean ones. You don't even know how to turn the hot water system on. The most important thing is to sleep, so from out of the chaos you manage to put up the bed and find some sheets and a quilt. Your head hits the pillow and you sigh gratefully – rest at last! However, you can hear all kinds of strange noises and you don't know what they are, so you lie awake with your brain turning somersaults. Eventually sleep overtakes you, and you have some vivid dreams - wondering if you have done the right thing, missing your old bedroom, tossing and turning, waking at times disturbed by the strange noises.

The next morning the sunlight pours through the window (where there are no curtains yet) and you wake up and stretch, wondering where you are. Then you remember, and happily you jump out of bed, knowing there is a long day and some hard work ahead.

By the time evening comes, your new house is beginning to look like a home, and you can shower and change, ready to go out for a nice meal to celebrate. You look around proudly at your new house, remembering all the effort you have had to make, and suddenly you *know* it has all been worth it!

Exercise 7.2
a) didn't know that.
b) We're going on holiday.
c) I've been away.
d) I couldn't do it.
e) It's time to go.
f) I think she's cute.
g) I think you'll know her.
h) We've forgotten something.
i) If he can, he'll get here.
j) They've been and gone.

Exercise 7.3
a) Paul's hair is very long
b) *The chef's skills are second to none. (If there was more than one chef, the apostrophe would go after the 's'.)*
c) The book's title is misleading.
d) I like driving my mother's car.
e) Have you ever been to one of Dee Young's performances?
f) We are nearly at our journey's end.
g) *The managers' rooms have been reserved. (If there was only one manager, the apostrophe would go before the 's'.)*
h) I have received the candidate's references. *(If there was more than candidate, the apostrophe would go after the 's'.)*
i) The men's race is about to begin.
j) The doctor's surgery is closed. *(If there was more than one doctor, the apostrophe would go after the 's'.)*

k) I enjoy reading women's magazines.
l) My granddad belonged to a Gentlemen's Club.
m) Percy Shaw invented reflecting road studs after seeing how cats' eyes lit up in the dark.
n) I don't understand that man's point of view.
o) All the workers' wages are really good.

Exercise 7.4
a) The book was given to John, so I think it is his.
b) This piece of land is shown on our deeds, so it must be ours.
c) A tiger can easily be recognised by the marks on its coat.
d) I found this coat in my car after giving you a lift, so I think it must be yours.
e) Holly insists that the trainers are hers.
f) The twins told me that the car is theirs to share at.

Exercise 7.5
a) I think it's going to rain.
b) It's the best thing I ever did.
c) The dog is wagging its tail.
d) It's only 8 o'clock.
e) Do you know what time it's starting?
f) Each house has its own garden.
g) I think it's going to be good.
h) The school has its own swimming pool.
i) A computer has its uses.
j) A good supermarket knows the needs of its customers.

Exercise 8.1
    a) "Do you want a lift?" he asked.
    b) "No thank you," I said.
    c) Abi commented to me, "It's very cold today."
    d) "My computer's not working," the woman said.
    e) Vikki said, "There aren't many people here."
    f) He hesitated before saying to me, "We'll have to set on more staff."

Exercise 8.2
    a) "Your car needs cleaning," the boy whispered.
    b) "You can't come in here," the manager said.
    c) Emma looked at me and said, "You haven't a leg to stand on."
    d) "The telephone's ringing," I pointed out.
    e) "Aren't you going to answer it?" I asked.
    f) My mother said, "It's your birthday next week."

Exercise 8.3
    a) "Rebecca," I said, "you're wearing a dress just like Jessica's."
    b) "If you go shopping," Josh said, "would you bring me a newspaper and a bar of chocolate?"
    c) "Don't do that!" I shouted. "You'll break it!"
    d) "The weather is fine," she said, "for ducks and fish."
    e) "You might be right," he said, "after all."
    f) "Shall I turn on the light?" I suggested. "Then we'll be able to see better."
    g) "Sorry," I told him. "I'm not interested."
    h) "Where there's muck," the old man said, "there's always money."

i) "I can't see properly," I told the optician. "I think I need a new pair of glasses."

j) "Well, well," Chloe said. "What do we have here?"

Exercise 8.4

a) The man told me he was "an old hand" at sailing a boat.

b) The writer tells us that Rigby's "best ever meal" was eaten on the cliff top.

c) He explained that the music is "a variant of jazz mixed with a bit of classical".

d) I remember, as a toddler, telling my mother that I was a "poor little girl".

e) The dentist told me I would have "a smile like a million dollars".

f) When your scores are equal you are said to have a "draw".

g) My grandmother told me there was "a pot of gold at the end of the rainbow".

Exercise 9.1

a) My father - the owner of the factory - is the best manager I know. (dashes, but could also be commas or brackets)

b) He is in his mid-forties. (hyphen)

c) Potatoes - my favourite food - can be cooked in a variety of ways. (dashes, but could also be commas)

d) I was talking to Mr King (the landlord) last night. (brackets, but could also be commas)

e) My grandfather was a soldier in the First World War (1914-1918). (brackets)

f) I have a multi-fuel burning stove. (hyphen)
g) Logs - which are in plentiful supply - are a cheap form of fuel. (dashes, but could also be commas)

Exercise 10.1
a) Ella is my half-sister; but no doubt you can see that. (semi-colon)
b) I tried to imagine the room painted in different colours: blue, pink, beige, lilac, white, cream, pale green. (colon)
c) The months of the year are: January, February, March, April…and so on, till December. (ellipses)
d) I can't tell you; that is the end of the story. (semi-colon)
e) Did you know that I'm…no, I don't suppose you do. (ellipses)
f) The buffet had sandwiches, pies, French bread, salad, samosas, cold meats, cheese…everything you could think of. (ellipses)
g) The winners of the show are: Rebecca, Stephanie and Simon. (colon)
h) I can't do it; you'll have to believe me. (semi-colon)

Exercise 11.1
Have you ever moved house? No? I have, several times, and I always wonder if I am mad to take on such a project. I will tell you why.

First of all, if you are buying a new property, you have to choose the house you want, which can take weeks or even months. Then, although the house has been put up for sale at a certain price, it is expected that you will make an offer. You decide how much you would *really* like to pay, put in your offer, and wait to see if it is accepted. Sometimes you have to increase the offer you have made, perhaps more than once. If you are selling a house at the same time, you have to have it valued, choose an estate agent, put it on the market, wait for the viewers to turn up...but we won't go into that.

Okay, let's assume that everything's going forward, you've agreed a final price on the house you are buying, and the legal aspects are going as smoothly as can be expected. There are many letters to answer, phone calls to make, e-mails to send, price adjustments regarding the condition of the house and the fixtures and fittings. As the big day approaches you have to pack up the entire contents of your home. You find things you thought you had lost. You need to throw away lots of rubbish. You have to decide what you are taking with you, and what you will get rid of. Eventually you are living out of boxes, with only the barest minimum of things not packed.

On the day of moving it is normal practice for you, your buyer and the person you are buying from all to move on the same day, so things must be planned with military precision. You can only hope that everything is all cleared out at your new home, and that it has been cleaned ready for you to move in. Luckily, your removal men arrive on time, and you watch your old house getting more and more empty.

By the end of the day everything has been shifted, and you sit at your new place amongst the boxes, wondering where you will put everything. You are hungry and tired, but you feel much too scruffy in your old clothes to go out for a meal, and you haven't a clue where to find some clean ones. You don't even know how to turn the hot water system on. The most important thing is to sleep, so from out of the chaos you manage to put up the bed and find some sheets and a quilt. Your head hits the pillow and you sigh gratefully – rest at last! However, you can hear all kinds of strange noises and you don't know what they are, so you lie awake with your brain turning somersaults. Eventually sleep overtakes you, and you have some vivid dreams - wondering if you have done the right thing, missing your old bedroom, tossing and turning, waking at times disturbed by the strange noises.

The next morning the sunlight pours through the window (where there are no curtains yet) and you wake up and stretch, wondering where you are. Then you remember, and happily you jump out of bed, knowing there is a long day and some hard work ahead.

By the time evening comes, your new house is beginning to look like a home, and you can shower and change, ready to go out for a nice meal to celebrate. You look around proudly at your new house, remembering all the effort you have had to make, and suddenly you *know* it has all been worth it!